Ben Ashley

Your Best Voice:

A Professional's Essential Guide to Vocal Excellence

Copyright © 2025 by Ben Ashley

All rights reserved.
No part of this publication may be reproduced, distributed, or transmitted in any form or by any means—electronic, mechanical, photocopying, recording, or otherwise—without the prior written permission of the author, except in the case of brief quotations used for reviews, educational purposes, or scholarly works.

Table of Contents

Introduction..9

Chapter 1: The Truth About Singing.............13

Chapter 2: The Singer's Foundation..............19

Chapter 3: Mastering Your Voice....................27

Chapter 4: Avoiding Common Mistakes.......37

Chapter 5: How to Practice Like a Pro..........49

Chapter 6: From the Stage to the Studio......59

Chapter 7: Keep the Momentum Going.........67

Cheat Sheets..73

Image Credits...95

About the Author..97

Introduction
Master Your Voice

Welcome to your journey toward vocal excellence.

Whether you're brand new to singing or looking to elevate your existing skills, this guide offers professional, practical techniques designed to unlock your true singing potential.

I'm Ben, a professional singer with years of experience performing live on television, along with an extensive background in vocal training and teaching. My mission is to help you build a robust vocal foundation, avoid common pitfalls, and develop techniques that have empowered singers I've coached—and myself—to thrive.

Throughout this guide, you'll gain access to clear strategies to enhance breath support, expand your vocal range, master your vocal capabilities, and confidently perform on stage and in the studio. Each chapter provides actionable insights, easy-to-follow exercises, and professional practices to elevate your singing abilities.

Your voice is powerful, unique, and ready to be discovered.

Let's embark on this exciting journey together!

Chapter 1: The Truth About Singing

If you've ever said "I wish I could sing," you're not alone. The world is full of people who believe singing is something you're either born with or not. And that belief? It's one of the biggest myths in music.

Singing is a skill. Like learning to ride a bike or speak a new language, it can be taught, practiced, improved, and mastered. Yes, some people may start with a natural ear or a pleasant voice—but without proper training, even naturally gifted singers reach limits quickly.

As a professional singer who has performed live on television and trained extensively, I can confidently tell you: the singers you admire didn't get there by accident. They trained, rehearsed, made mistakes, and grew from them. And you can too.

Talent is a Starting Point, not a Destination

Natural talent helps—but it's no substitute for technique, consistency, and discipline. I've worked with incredibly gifted singers who lacked stamina or control because they never built a solid foundation. I've also seen beginners with average voices transform into outstanding performers through proper training and dedication.

Your voice is a muscle. Just like going to the gym, the more you train it correctly, the stronger, and more flexible it becomes.

Why Most People Get Singing Wrong

There are three main reasons people struggle with singing:

1. They don't breathe correctly.
2. They force or push their voice instead of supporting it.
3. They try to copy others instead of discovering their own natural voice.

This book is about changing those habits. I'll guide you through the techniques I use—and teach others—to sing freely, powerfully, and without strain.

Whether you're starting fresh or overcoming old habits, this book gives you the mindset and methods to make real, measurable progress.

No shortcuts. Just expert, professional vocal coaching that gets results

Let's begin building your foundation.

Chapter 2: The Singer's Foundation

Before we jump into fancy techniques or vocal tricks, we need to get something straight: your voice can only go as far as your foundation allows. If your breath support is weak or your posture is working against you, you'll always feel like you're fighting your own body.

Let's fix that.

Posture: Your First Instrument

Your voice doesn't start in your throat—it starts in your body.

When your body is aligned, your lungs can expand fully, your diaphragm can move freely, and your sound flows naturally.
Here's a quick checklist to get into proper singing posture:

- Stand tall, feet hip-width apart
- Knees soft (not locked)
- Shoulders relaxed and down
- Chest slightly lifted
- Head level, not tilted forward

If you're sitting, use a firm chair and sit upright—not slouched on a sofa. Imagine a string gently pulling the crown of your head upward. You're setting your body up to sing, not to scroll through your phone.

Breath Support: The Power Behind Your Voice

Breath is everything. Without proper breath support, your voice won't have power, control, or stamina.
You've probably heard the term "sing from your diaphragm." That's true—but what does it actually mean?

The diaphragm is a muscle that sits below your lungs. When you inhale deeply, the diaphragm moves downward, allowing your lungs to expand and fill with air. When you exhale (or sing), the diaphragm helps control the release of that air.

Most people breathe shallowly, using just their chest or shoulders. That causes tension and forces the vocal cords to work harder than they should.

The Simple Way to Train Diaphragmatic Breathing

Try this right now:

1. Lie flat on your back and place one hand on your stomach and one on your chest.
2. Take a slow breath in through your nose.
3. Feel your stomach rise. Your chest should stay mostly still.
4. Exhale through your mouth slowly, feeling your stomach fall.

That's diaphragmatic breathing.

Once you feel it lying down, try it standing. Place your hands on your sides—where your ribs are—and aim to feel expansion there when you inhale.

With time, this becomes second nature—and it's the key to controlled, supported singing.

A Daily Breath Warm-Up (2 Minutes)
1. Inhale for 4 counts
2. Hold your breath for 4 counts — but don't use your throat to hold it. Keep your throat relaxed and hold the air in your lungs. Your vocal cords should stay loose.
3. Exhale on a hiss (sssssss) for 8 counts
4. Repeat, increasing the exhale time to 10, then 12, then 16

This simple exercise builds control, focus, and lung capacity—without tension. It's one of the most important things you can do before any singing session.

Foundation First

If you can stand tall, breathe deeply, and stay relaxed, you've already taken a massive step toward singing like a professional.

The techniques in the next chapters will build on this—but this is the root. Without it, everything else crumbles.

Take your time with this. Revisit it often. Your voice will thank you.

Chapter 3: Mastering Your Voice

Now that you've got the foundation—good posture, proper breath support, and a calm, relaxed body—you're ready to start shaping your sound.

This is where we begin to "unlock" your voice. Not by forcing it or copying someone else, but by developing your own natural tone, learning control, and discovering the full range of what your voice can do.

Step 1: Know Your Vocal Range

Your vocal range is the span from your lowest note to your highest usable note. Understanding this helps you choose songs that suit you and practice more effectively.

As a tenor, I can tell you: knowing your range is about more than hitting high notes—it's about knowing where your voice shines.

To find your range:

- Sit at a keyboard or use a piano app.
- Start humming your lowest comfortable note.
- Gradually move up, note by note, until you can no longer sing without straining.
- Do the same in reverse to find your upper and lower limits.

You don't need to force anything. Your voice will develop with time and technique.

Step 2: Understand the Vocal Registers

You have three main vocal registers:

- Chest Voice – Your speaking voice. Rich, full, strong.
- Head Voice – Lighter, higher tone. Often used for high notes or softer sounds.
- Mixed Voice – A blend of chest and head. This is the key to singing powerfully without shouting.

Many beginners try to carry chest voice too far up or head voice too far down. The result? Tension and strain. The trick is learning to blend them—something we'll work on together.

Step 3: Vocal Placement & Resonance

Where you "place" your voice in your body changes the tone.

Try this:

- Hum gently and feel where the vibration is.
- Now say "mm-hmm" like you agree with someone.
- Feel that buzz in your lips or your face? That's forward placement—great for singing.

You want your voice to resonate in your mask (the area around your nose, mouth, and cheekbones) rather than in the throat or chest.

The more your voice resonates forward, the more efficient it becomes—and the better it sounds with less effort.

Step 4: The Mirror Rule

Get comfortable practicing in front of a mirror. Why? Because awareness is key.

- Are your shoulders rising when you breathe?
- Are you tensing your neck or jaw when singing higher notes?
- Is your mouth open enough for sound to travel freely?

The mirror doesn't lie. It's one of your most powerful practice tools.

Step 5: Daily Tone Exercise (5 Minutes)

Here's a simple daily warm-up to build tone and vocal placement:

- Lip trills (or tongue trills) going from low to high and back down — gentle and smooth
- Sirens on an "ng" sound (as in "sing") — stretch your range without force
- "Nay-nay-nay" on a 5-note scale — forward, slightly bratty tone helps train mixed voice

Do this gently. Your voice should feel relaxed and resonant—not tight.

You're Starting to Sing Like a Pro

This is the fun part—exploring your voice and learning what it can really do.

Don't worry if it doesn't sound "perfect" yet. It's not about perfection—it's about progress, day by day.

With each practice, you're building the coordination, awareness, and confidence that professional singers rely on every time they step on stage.

In the next chapter, we'll talk about the most common mistakes that hold singers back—and how to avoid them for good.

Chapter 4: Avoiding Common Mistakes

Even with a solid foundation and growing technique, many singers hit a wall—not because they lack talent, but because of a few key habits that quietly sabotage progress.

These mistakes are incredibly common—even among professionals early in their careers. The good news? Once you're aware of them, you can correct them and improve fast.

Mistake 1: Pushing for Power

A lot of singers think more volume equals better singing, so they push harder—especially on high notes.

The result? Strain, tension, and eventually damage.

Singing powerfully has very little to do with force. Real power comes from breath control, resonance, and proper placement—not shouting.

If your neck tightens or your face scrunches up when you go for a note, you're muscling it instead of supporting it. Pull back. Refocus on breath.

Mistake 2: Neglecting Warm-Ups

You wouldn't sprint cold or lift weights without warming up. Your voice is no different.

Singing without warming up can cause:

- Pitch instability
- Vocal fatigue
- Long-term vocal strain

Even 5 minutes of warm-ups can completely change the quality and ease of your singing. Make it part of your ritual—even if you're just singing along to the radio.

(We'll include a warm-up cheat sheet at the end of this eBook.)

Mistake 3: Trying to Sound Like Someone Else

It's natural to admire great singers. But the goal isn't to become them—it's to become the best version of you.

Trying to mimic tone, vibrato, or placement that doesn't suit your voice usually leads to tension and frustration.

Instead, ask:

- What do I like about their sound?
- How can I use that influence while staying true to my voice?

Some of the most powerful voices in the world weren't traditionally "pretty"—they were unique, authentic, and emotionally connected.

Mistake 4: Overthinking Every Note

Once you start learning technique, it's easy to fall into analysis paralysis.

"Was that note supported?"
"Did I use enough mix?"
"Was my larynx too high?"

Stop. Take a breath. Sing.

Think technique during warm-ups and practice—but when it's time to perform (even just for yourself), let go. Trust the work you've done and focus on the story you're telling.

Mistake 5: Inconsistent Practice

You don't need hours a day. But you do need consistency.

15 minutes a day is better than 2 hours once a week. Regular practice builds muscle memory and coordination—and slowly reshapes how your voice works.

Here's a simple commitment:

- 3–5 days a week
- Warm-up → tone & range exercises → sing a song you love
- Track how it feels, not just how it sounds

Over time, you'll notice clearer tone, easier high notes, and greater control.

Progress Comes from Awareness, Not Perfection

You're going to make mistakes. Every singer does. The difference is whether you learn from them or let them frustrate you.

Every voice is different, and your journey won't look like anyone else's. But if you stay consistent, pay attention, and avoid these common traps—you'll grow faster than you think.

In the next chapter, we'll build a daily practice routine that fits your life and helps you build real momentum.

A Story from the Stage

I'll never forget the first night I performed at BBC Television Centre London
There were 10 million people watching on the other side of that camera. I'd done loads of shows. But this was something else. It wasn't nerves—it was a tidal wave of "what ifs."

And then I remembered something so simple
Just breathe. One proper, deep, low breath. Not a panic breath—a singer's breath.

Everything settled.

I walked out, hit the first note, and from that moment on—it was just me and the music.

That night reminded me of something I always say:
You don't need to be fearless—you just need to be ready.

Carrie Grant giving last-minute advice before going live.*

Live interview with Fearne Cotton during BBC's Children in Need broadcast*.

Performing live to a studio audience, broadcast to over 10 million viewers*

With Ruthie Henshall while working together on ITV

My vocal coach, Carrie.

Performing live at the O2 Arena, London.

Chapter 5: How to Practice Like a Pro

Most singers don't get stuck because they're untalented. They get stuck because they don't know how to practice.

It's not about singing for hours and hoping for the best—it's about being intentional. Professional singers don't just sing—they rehearse with purpose, focus, and structure.

This chapter will show you how to practice efficiently, stay motivated, and make consistent progress—whether you have 15 minutes or a full hour.

The Three-Part Practice Formula

Every solid practice session includes these three elements:

1. Warm-Up – to activate the breath, stretch the range, and prep the voice

2. Technique Work – where the real skill-building happens

3. Application – singing a song or phrase with your new awareness

Let's break that down.

Part 1: Warm-Up (5–10 Minutes)

Start every session with a simple, structured warm-up. This gets your breath moving, relaxes the vocal cords, and gently eases your voice into action.

Try this sequence:

- Lip trills (make siren sounds from low to high)

- "ng" slides (from low to high and back down)

- Humming on a 5-note scale

- Short phrases like "gee-gee-gee" or "nay-nay-nay" for forward placement

Always use light pressure. You're waking up the voice—not pushing it.

Part 2: Technique Work (10–15 Minutes)

Example exercises:

- "Ma-ma-ma" on an arpeggio (that's when you sing the notes of a chord one at a time, like a stair-step pattern going up and down—great for building pitch control and clarity)

- Long sustained notes on a hiss or vowel for breath control

- "Mum-mum-mum" from low to high for mixed voice

- Working on register transitions with vowel shaping

Part 3: Application (5–15 Minutes)

Pick a song you love—or a challenging phrase—and apply what you just practiced.

Don't just sing it through blindly. Break it down:

- Where are you running out of breath?

- Is a certain word forcing tension?

- Could a vowel modification make it easier?

Practice in sections, repeat phrases, then bring it all together.

This is where singing becomes expressive again—not just technical. It's also where breakthroughs happen.

Weekly Structure (Suggested Schedule)

Day	Focus
Mon	Breath support + warm-up
Tue	Resonance + vocal placement
Wed	Mixed voice + bridging
Thu	Application: song practice
Fri	High notes + register work
Sat	Rest or light warm-up only
Sun	Free sing / record & reflect

If five or six days feels like too much—start with three. It's better to be consistent three days a week than to do six once and give up.

Track Your Progress

Keep a small practice journal or voice memo log. Each time you rehearse, note:

- What you worked on

- How it felt

- What improved

- What needs more focus

This builds self-awareness and shows how far you've come. And on days when motivation dips, looking back at how much you've grown can re-ignite your drive.

Practice Is the Secret

You don't need to be perfect. You just need to be consistent.

The singers you admire didn't get there overnight. They put in the reps, made mistakes, learned, and kept showing up.

And now—it's your turn.

In the next chapter, we'll shift gears and look at performing. Because sounding great in your room is one thing—but learning how to sing in front of others is a skill all its own.

Chapter 6: From the Stage to the Studio

Singing in your room is one thing. Singing in front of an audience, or into a studio microphone, is something else entirely.

You can have a great voice—but if nerves take over or you don't understand how to manage your energy in performance, your technique can fall apart.

This chapter is about preparing your voice, your mind, and your presence—so when it's time to perform, you deliver with confidence and control.

Performing Live: What It Takes

I've sung live on national television in front of 10 million people. You don't get a second take. Here's what that taught me:

- You don't need to be fearless—you just need to be prepared.
- Confidence comes from repetition, not ego.
- Nerves are normal. What matters is how you manage them.

If you're breathing properly, staying grounded, and connecting emotionally with the song—you're doing it right.

Here are a few practical tips:

- Do your vocal warm-up, no matter how short the set
- Ground yourself—feel your feet, breathe low
- Focus on the message of the song, not yourself
- Rehearse like it's the real thing. The more you've practiced with intensity, the more natural it'll feel when it counts

Mental Preparation: Replacing Nerves with Intention

Nerves don't mean you're not ready. They mean you care.

Here's a trick I still use:

When you feel that surge of adrenaline, tell yourself: "My body is helping me focus." That energy is there to sharpen you, not sabotage you.

Also, never rehearse only physically. Visualize. Mentally walk through the song. Picture the room, the lights, your breath. This conditions your brain and body to feel safe in performance.

Stage Presence: Being Seen and Felt

You don't have to dance or move wildly to have stage presence. Sometimes the most powerful moments come from stillness.
Here's how to build natural stage presence:

- Know your lyrics so well that you can focus on the emotion
- Open your body—avoid folding your arms or retreating into yourself
- Make eye contact if you can
- Let the emotion lead your expression, not the other way around

Remember: people aren't just listening to your voice—they're experiencing your energy.

Studio Singing: Different Rules, Same Voice

The studio environment is a different beast. It's quiet. Controlled. Every detail is captured.

Here's what matters most when recording vocals:

- Stay relaxed—don't push
- Use consistent breath support
- Be aware of plosives (hard consonants like "p" and "b")—pull slightly back from the mic
- Use headphones to monitor your pitch and blend
- Don't aim for perfection in one take—layering and emotion matter more than flawless pitch

And this is key:

In the studio, your emotions can be felt—even through the smallest nuance. You don't need to belt to move someone. You just need to connect with the song.

If you mean what you're singing, the mic will pick it up. Aim for sincerity, not just sound.

Whether It's One Person or Ten Thousand…
The principles stay the same:
- Breathe
- Support
- Focus on connection

Your technique gives you the freedom to express. Your preparation gives you the confidence to perform.

In the next (and final) chapter, we'll talk about where to go from here—and how to continue growing, whether you're heading for the stage, the studio, or simply your best personal voice.

Chapter 7: Keep the Momentum Going

Growth comes from repetition and curiosity. The more you explore your voice with patience and purpose, the more it will open up.

Keep showing up to practice—even when your motivation dips. Especially then.

Sing songs that move you. Keep a vocal journal. Record yourself every few weeks and listen back without judgment—only awareness.

Your voice will keep evolving as long as you stay connected to it.

Build Your Confidence, Brick by Brick

Confidence doesn't come from being perfect. It comes from knowing that you've put in the work—and learning to trust yourself in the moment.

Even the pros have shaky rehearsals and off-days. What sets them apart is that they keep going. They lean into their technique, and they remind themselves: "I've done this before. I can do it again."

Surround Yourself with Support

If you want to go further, faster—get feedback.

Whether it's from a coach, a trusted musician, or a fellow singer who understands the process, outside ears help you grow in ways you can't always see for yourself.

And if you ever feel stuck, remember: the best singers in the world are still students.

Vocal Training Cheat Sheets

Cheat Sheet 1: Daily Vocal Warm-Up

Title: 5-Minute Professional Vocal Warm-Up

Use this routine before singing—whether you're rehearsing, recording, or going on stage.

Step 1: Posture Check (30 sec)

Stand tall, feet hip-width apart

Knees relaxed, chest lifted

Shoulders down, neck relaxed

Head level—not tilted up or down

→ Breathe freely and gently into your belly

Step 2: Breath Activation (1 min)

Inhale for 4 counts

Hold breath for 4 counts (use your lungs, not your throat!)

Exhale on a steady hiss "ssss" for 8 counts

Repeat 3x

→ Increase exhale time gradually (10, 12, 16 counts)

Step 3: Vocal Warm-Up Sequence (3–4 min)

Lip Trills (sirens) – glide from low to high, back down

"ng" Slides (as in "sing") – gentle slides through your range

5-Note Scale on "Gee-gee-gee" – bright, forward tone

"Nay-nay-nay" – slightly bratty voice for resonance & mix

Stay light—don't push or force volume

Keep your face and jaw relaxed

Feel the sound resonate forward (not in the throat)

Do this daily to build coordination, breath control & tone

Cheat Sheet 2:

Weekly Practice Tracker

Title: Your Weekly Singing Practice Plan

Track your progress, stay consistent, and build your voice over time.

Weekly Goals

This week, I want to focus on improving:

Optional: My song focus this week is:

Daily Practice Log

Day	Warm-Up Done?	Technique Focus	Song Practiced	Notes / Feelings After Practice
Monday	☐			
Tuesday	☐			
Wednesday	☐			
Thursday	☐			
Friday	☐			
Saturday	☐			
Sunday	☐			

Reflection

What felt better this week?

What do I want to work on next week?

Bonus Tip: Even 3–4 consistent days per week makes a huge difference. Singing is a muscle—build it little by little.

Cheat Sheet 3:

Vocal Range Finder & Register Guide

Title: Discover Your Vocal Range

Find your natural range, understand your registers, and start singing within your sweet spot.

Step 1: Find Your Range

You'll need a keyboard (real or app), or a

vocal range finder tool online.

Start humming your lowest comfortable note.

Move upward, note by note, until your voice naturally "lifts" or breaks.

Keep going carefully until your highest usable note (without strain).

Do the same going down from the middle.

Write down your vocal range using note names (e.g., C3 – A4).

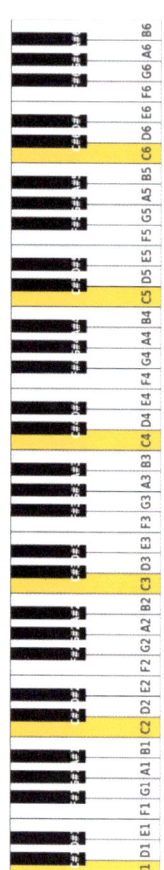

My range:

Lowest comfortable note: _____

Highest usable note: _____

Step 2: Identify Your Registers

Your voice moves through three main registers:

Register	Description	Feels Like...
Chest Voice	Full, rich, speaking-range tone	Strong, grounded, natural
Mixed Voice	Blend of chest and head	Balanced, forward, smooth
Head Voice	Lighter, higher tone (often airy at first)	Floaty, bright, lifted

Tip: There's no perfect "line" between them. Blending takes time—don't rush or strain.

Step 3: Sing in the Right Key

Pick songs that fit well within your current range. As your voice grows, your range will expand naturally.

Quick check:

- Does the song sit mostly in your chest/mix?

- Are you straining to hit the high notes?

- Could you transpose it slightly to feel more comfortable?

Bonus Tip: Your voice might sound different as you train—that's normal.

As you develop control and resonance, your range and tone will evolve.

Cheat Sheet 4: The Daily Breath Builder

Title: 2-Minute Breathing Boost for Singers

Train your breath like a singer—build control, stamina, and support with this simple daily routine.

What You'll Need

A timer (or count in your head)

A quiet space to focus

Optional: metronome (60–80 bpm is a good starting point)

Warm-Up Sequence: Breath Control Drill

Inhale deeply through your nose for 4 counts

Hold your breath for 4 counts (keep your throat relaxed—hold in the lungs)

Exhale on a steady hiss: "ssssss…" for 8 counts

Repeat the full cycle 3–4 times

→ As you improve, gradually increase the hiss count to 10, 12, and even 16 or 20

→ Stay relaxed in the shoulders, chest, and jaw throughout

Bonus: Place one hand on your belly and one on your chest. Your belly should rise as you inhale—chest stays mostly still.

Advanced Add-On: Breath Pulsing

Inhale for 4 counts

Exhale in short, controlled pulses: "ss-ss-ss-ss" in rhythm

Start with 4 pulses, then 8, then 12 (stay even and relaxed)

This helps with vocal agility, endurance, and phrase control in songs.

Daily breath training improves tone, pitch stability, and vocal confidence.

Just 2 minutes a day adds up to a more powerful, supported voice.

Final Thought

Your voice is a part of you. It's not just notes and technique—it's emotion, identity, and energy.

Take care of it. Be patient with it. And most of all—enjoy the process of discovering what it can do.

Because when you sing from a place of truth and connection, people feel it.

And that's what it's all about.

I'll see you in the next chapter of your journey.

Want More?

This book is just the beginning.

If you're ready to take the next step, I invite you to explore my full vocal training program—a structured course that walks you through everything I've learned in 25+ years of performing, recording, and teaching.

Inside, I go deeper into:

- Developing a professional-quality tone
- Expanding your range safely
- Mastering breath control and endurance
- Singing confidently on stage or in the studio
- Building a practice plan tailored to your goals

You can also get access to bonus video lessons, warm-ups, and feedback opportunities.

If you're ready to go further with your voice, I'd love to help you get there.

For more details, visit **www.masteryourvocal.com**

Image Credits

- All personal photos taken by the author, unless otherwise stated.

- *Photo of live performance at the O2 Arena* © Andrew Benge. Used with permission.

- *Photo(s) featuring Ruthie Henshall and Carrie Grant* taken by the author. Used with permission.

- *Live performance, interview with Fearne Cotton, on stage moments with Carrie Grant from BBC's Children in Need, 2005* — reproduced as editorial stills from the original television broadcast. *

*Some images are reproduced from original broadcasts for illustrative, editorial purposes. All rights remain with the original copyright holders. No endorsement is implied by any individuals or organisations depicted.

About the Author

Ben Ashley is a British vocalist who has been singing live for over 25 years across Europe—on stage, in studios, and on television—including a nationally broadcast performance seen by over 10 million viewers.

Known for his powerful, emotive vocals and deep connection to his craft, Ben has worked alongside celebrities and appeared on BBC's Children in Need and ITV's Britian Sing Christmas.

Having trained professionally and performed everything from musical theatre to classical crossover, Ben now focuses on passing that experience on to others. His goal is to help singers unlock their full potential with practical, proven techniques rooted in real-world performance.

This book is your first step toward building your best voice—and there's much more to come!

www.masteryourvocal.com

Printed in Dunstable, United Kingdom